SMART KIDS
SMART MONEY

The Ultimate Parent's Guide To Teaching Kids About Earning, Saving, Giving, Spending And Investing Money Wisely

LUCY LOVE

ISBN: 9781520358673

TABLE OF CONTENT

INTRODUCTION

Thank you and congratulate you for downloading my book on *"Smart Kids Smart Money: The Ultimate Parent's Guide To Teaching Kids About Earning, Saving, Giving, Spending And Investing Money Wisely."*

As parents, we are the first teachers who our children influence and learn a lot from whether directly or indirectly. The vast majority want our children to have tools to be successful when they grow up. We want to equip them with the best knowledge about financial literacy when they are still young. We want to teach them skills on how to save, manage, spend and invest money wisely as well. Apparently, kids will learn better at their early age because their mind will not be interrupted by life issues. As parents, therefore, we should take advantage of this period and teach our kids about money today.

This book will provide you proven steps, strategies, practical activities and powerful tips on how to instill your children about the concept of money, the value of hard work, the skills of managing and spending money wisely. This book will also guide you how to teach your kids about the willingness of giving money and helping others. It also offers you great tips on how to teach your children using credit cards efficiently and how to lead them to become wiser spenders when they grow up. All great tips and information are available inside.

Start teaching your kids on how to earn money today and you will be surprised with the outcome they will bring to their future life.

I hope you enjoy reading!

Thank you again for downloading this book!

Why Parents Should Instill Their Children About Money?

Parents might be thinking that their children are too young to learn about money. However, the truth is that it is never too early for parents to begin teaching money lessons for their children, especially when prices of everything in the modern time keep going up while the buyers receive less value than what they expected.

Why is it important to teach our kids learning about money matter at their early age? Let's look at a list of reasons as below:

Reason 1: Kids will be more likely to listen to their parents when they are at early ages. Why? Since they have yet to hit the maturity period; the period that they want to be independent and responsible for everything. Therefore, the entire process of teaching kids about money at this time would be much easier for parents. The kids will become more cooperative and obedient to us. Also, conversations and co-operations between parents and children in this period are much more open and easier to take place rather than when they grow up.

Reason 2: At an early age, the kids will seem to be less influenced by society and peer pressures. Obviously, parents are the child's significant influence in this period as they interact with us all the time. They will witness, supervise and imitate what we do or reacts. Therefore, as parents who are considered as the kid's first teachers, we must be wise and careful with every single thing we do in front of them. Don't wait until kids grow up and teach them about money matters. This is not effective at all only because the more children grow up, the more they will become affected and influenced by what school, teachers, peers, social media, and other people around teach them. What they are learning from such individuals in that environment are not always what we wish. As an outcome, it will become tougher for us as parents to teach our kids best knowledge while they prioritize what they learn from other sources.

Reason 3: When kids are still young, they can remember and apply the basics of what we teach easily and quickly due to their sharp brain and memory. They will imitate what we do excellently, and then, of course, they will partly lay a firm foundation for their characters when they grow up. Also, as parents, we will have more chance to interact with our kids, understand them better when they are still young. Find out what are their skills and flaws through the games or lessons they play and do together with us; then we can know which jobs are suitable for them and orient them to choose the right career when they grow up. This time is perfect for us as parents to discover our kid's natural talent, hobbies, what they like, what they dislike, etc.

Reason 4: The earlier we teach our children about money concept, guide them on how to save, manage, spend, and invest money, the sooner they will become conscious and wiser; they will start saving, and of course they will have a larger budget to use in future.

Reason 5: The earlier the kids have a chance to interact with money, make mistakes in spending and investing money, the fewer risks they will take in future. For me, as a parent, I would rather my kids make more mistakes in using money when they are at an early age rather than they will make mistakes and take risks when they grow up.

Reason 6: The earlier we teach our children about money, the sooner we will help them become happier and healthier. We obviously know that money plays a crucial role in our life. It helps us a lot for everything. Without money, we will probably face many problems in life. For example, problems about health, problems about relationships, issues about finance, etc. And challenges, of course, will increase pressure to us, and this will result in lacking happiness in our lives. Pressure about money can also increase the risk of many serious diseases we may suffer from such as heart disease, insomnia, migraines, and even mental disease. Therefore, it would be better if we equip our kids the best knowledge about money earlier so they would have the right attitude about money, they will know how to use money in the right way, how to spend and invest it wisely, then they will have a better life in future.

Teaching Children about the Concept and Value of Money

Teaching kids about money sound hard. However, as parents, we should allow our children to spend all of the money that they'd been collecting over early years. We want them to know what they felt like to not have any money and then, in turn, they will know how to save and spend money wisely afterward.

To be honest parents, it's hard to teach our young kids how to use money and how to spend it. The concept of money is so general because they see us use debit cards and credit cards all the time, right? It's very rare that they see us use cash, and when we do, they don't quite grasp the subject or how money works. Therefore, we must teach our kids with practical knowledge about money in reality.

In fact, children would learn better if their parents know how to make the lessons about the concept and value of money more attractive through stories or games. As a parent, therefore, you should create and play some simple games with the kids related to money, coins, notes, check, etc. For instance, do with your children in the store, you need to teach them how to learn the value of money. Teach them how to use it, how to earn it and how to spend it. The first thing you want to do is have your kids cash in their coins so you can easily see how much money they have.

Let your kids start with the Coin Star machine, teach them how to count all their pennies, having them be hands on, touch the screen, show the machine counting their money, etc. this way will help the kids see what's going on and interact with the experience of money. Get them to see the number get higher and higher on the screen. Then give them the cash receipt from Coin Star machine and make sure the cashier hands your child physically the cash so they can see the money in their hand and watch it leave when they pay for their items. As parents, you should give your young child a chance to see the money physically moving or they don't get the concept.

Also, you can also tell the kids successful stories about millionaires, billionaires who knew how to make money since they were a child like Warren Buffett, Steve Job, Bill Gate, etc. Teaching the kids what money is, why people need it, how great money helps people in life. Let them know that money is necessary and it should be used in the right way. Teach the kids that don't ever waste any penny. Explaining to them most of the things in life must be paid with money. Nearly nothing is free, from cars, houses, clothing, food, drinks, study tools until other things in life. Then we let them know that money requires us to work hard, it doesn't grow on trees, we must create it, respect it and treasure it as well. Teach the kids to work for money. That means you need to help the kids do chores, have them do household chores to earn money around the house. I will say that my little boy Danny was only three and a half, and he was doing chores.

So if you have little kids like I do, then allow them to do chores. They can dust, go around and clean all of the doorknobs. That's what little kids can do. They can think that doing chores is quite fun. You will probably find it interesting that your little kids may love to help their older siblings' clean things or do other small tasks because they want to be like the bigger kids. So it's rather helpful to put our children to work, right?

And the important thing I want to share with you that as parents, you have to do with sticking to your goals. You have to stick to your goals.

Sometimes, your kids will be like, *"Oh mom, I'll pay you money back later"* Or *"I'll do the job later, but I want money now."* It's like you're giving them a reward before they've done the work. And little kids' minds don't work that way. So you have to make sure that they do the job first, and then they'll see the reward. You must try hard not to give into your kid's needs.

Teach the kids about the basic concepts of money. Doing so will help them lay a strong foundation for their financial habits once they become adults.

Explaining The Basics Of Money Terms to Children

When your child reaches an appropriate age, teach him/her about the basic terms of money so they would have a general understanding of the financial world. Here is a list of financial terms you should let your kids know:

1. **CHECK:** it is a piece of paper that you order the bank to pay a specific amount of money from your bank account to the person in whose name the check has been written.

2. **CREDIT:** it is the trust which allows one party (lender) to provide money or resources to another party (borrower). If the borrower repays the money on time, he/she will obtain an excellent credit and have a high chance to borrow an amount of money at a low-interest rate.

3. **INTEREST:** it is a payment which is done by a borrower to a lender for an amount of money above repayment of the original sum of the borrowed money. It is also considered as a fee which the borrower may pay the lender for borrowing money.

4. **DIVIDEND:** it is a yearly, bi-annually, or quarterly payment made by a corporation to its shareholders, usually as a distribution of profits.

5. **A MUTUAL FUND**: investment enterprises operate it. It is a professionally fared investment fund that collects money from many investors to purchase securities/stocks.

6. **SAVING ACCOUNT:** it is an account maintained by a retail financial organization (a bank or credit union) that pays interest on the money people deposit, but it cannot be used directly as money in the constricted sense of a medium of exchange.

7. **STOCK:** when you own stock in a company, it means you own an ownership in the business that issues the security. As an owner, you will have the right to receive a dividend or a portion of the company's profits. On the other hand, if the company loses money, then you will receive or earn nothing, and of course, the value of the stock goes down.

Breaking Down the Expenses and Amount of Items

If you want your children to become wiser about money matters, as parents, you must equip your children with knowledge of expenditures for things. Tell them that almost everything costs money. Nothing is free. To provide your children with the best knowledge of fees, you should increase your knowledge first by reading more books, magazines, news, sites, and then give your kids the best tips and advice on how to expense for things effectively in their daily life. If you know that your son likes a car, you should analyze the pros and cons of owning a car. For example, you can tell them how much car costs, what fees we have to pay when we use a car (tax, gas, toll fee, parking space, etc..) likewise. You can also tell them the benefits when we have a car; then you conclude that the disadvantages outweigh the advantages when they own a car they don't have a lot of money. Instead, you should encourage them to use that amount of money to invest into stock, dividends, real estate; they will get a chance to earn more money and become rich in future. Likewise, you can also teach your child to save money by eating at home instead of eating at restaurants since everything in restaurants is much more expensive.

Instill the Value of Hard – Earned Money to Children

Work hard and be rewarded

Don't let our children stick into a bad habit of waiting until the last minutes and ask us for money. At their early age, they obviously don't know how hard we work for the money. They just think that we are a cash machine, and money always comes from us. They believe that we are always ready when they need money for snacks or toys.

When teaching kids, we should let them know that we have to work hard to get money. Explain to them that money doesn't come quickly, it requires us to work for it. Money doesn't come from the parents as well, and it doesn't come from the trees either. Let them know we are not a money machine.

Teach children that when they work hard, they will be rewarded in return. Note that we must make the topic more interesting by telling them several hard-work stories for kids like the story of the ant. In this story, the ant even though small, but they are diligent, they keep themselves working all day to collect food, build the house, and prepare everything for the coming winter. On the other hand, we should also tell the kids adverse consequences that independent individuals may suffer from if they are lazy like having no food to eat, no clothes to wear, no houses to stay and particularly we will have no money to help people who are in need. We can take the character grasshopper in the story as an example of this. In the story, the character grasshopper is so lazy; he just spends time playing guitar all day without working hard, when the winter comes, he has nothing to support himself but asking the ants for a favor. The story will help the kids feel more interested in learning from it. They will have more fun and can learn about the values of working hard in life as well. Let them know that working hard will not only help us create happiness, meet our basic daily needs such as food, clothes, houses, but help us know about the value of earning money. These things, of course, make us survive and grow. Also, hard work also allows kids to have a chance to earn money and buy whatever they like such as gun toys, bicycles, dolls, etc. Teach the kids that through working hard, we will learn a lot of new things, get more experiences and become smarter in life.

Make clear to the kids that they will always get rewards for their hard work; motivate them to take action, do more chores, giving and being helpful to others more often. Like I said, remember that we must be rewarding the kids for the work they complete as we promised. It doesn't matter how the work they do, where the work is done as long as they deserve to pay when they complete all these things.

Encourage the kids to do chores is an excellent way to help them work hard and develop their life skills at the early age. Assign them four to five tasks with the understanding that they must work hard if they want to get a reward. The jobs we offer them should be suitable for their ages, hobbies such as collecting rubbish, picking up toys, cleaning the house, preparing food for the family, washing dishes, etc.

Note that children will become smarter and more successful in life if they have a chance to interact with money and develop their skills since they were still young. As parents, we should encourage our kids taking more action since we know that the more they do, the more they learn, the earlier they take risks, the sooner they will be successful. This is a great technique for parents to teach their kids about money.

Commission vs. Allowance

As a parent, we should reward our child with a commission instead of an allowance. An allowance just means an amount of money that is enough for our child's daily expenses. That is the price that we pay our kid each day or each week. Also, a commission will get our children become more excited and hard-working if they want to get rewards.

The allowance is significant. It is the gateway of budgeting. It will teach the kids how to set boundaries when it comes to money. Compensation pay to a child not for money but actual expenses. This means the child probably reach at the age of seven or eight before you introduce an allowance.

To be straightforward, you get a piece of paper, talk about the expenses in your child life and help them take charge of all of such expenditures, maybe their lunch at school and then give them that money to manage over a period. Everything needs to be done in an appropriate way. At first, give them one week allowance to handle and tell them that they can use the money to spend for lunch at school, or they can keep it by eating at home during break time. Start giving your children choices when it comes to money, and allowance is a great way to start to give kids options.

Research shows that parents should allow their children get a "commission," instead of an allowance, for doing certain chores. Sometimes, we can require them to do general housework without payment. Let them know that we do so simply because they are parts of the family.

Why do parents do this way? Because in real life, we only get paid for what we are hired to do. In contrast, we will get no payment for things that we have to do since we are part of a family or community. Teach our kids that if they want to get paid, they must work for it. For example, you tell them to pick up litter to keep the city clean, or help parents do chores at home, then you pay them as a commission.

Why don't we give them an allowance? The truth is revealed that if parents give their kid an allowance for doing chores, it does not help them learn how to make money and they will lose the chance of learning the lessons from working to make their money.

Chore Ideas

To help our kids have a chance of getting a commission, we should create a list of chores and select those fit our child's age and ability.

You can ask your kids what chores they would like to do. You may be surprised when you get their choices. This way will help you know exactly what your child can do and what they "like" doing.

To help our children have a chance to make extra money, we should make a list of additional chores

Here is the list of tasks we can get our children started:

- Make bedroom: $1
- Set table: $1
- Sweep floors: $1
- Vacuum: $1
- Water flowers/ plants: $2
- Clean the toilets: $2
- Empty the trash bins: $1
- Have the dog a bath: $2
- Mow the lawn: $5

Remember that we can break the big tasks down. This is a great method if your kid is still little. This will enable them to manage their tasks effectively. You don't need to have the kid do the entire chore, like clean the entire the house. Instead, we can allow them to do part of it.

After they select the chores, you set a reasonable value to them. Note that you must keep a promise to pay them right after they complete their work. Furthermore, if you see your kids do the chores excellently, you can give them more tips as a reward for their excellent performance.

Teaching Financial Responsibilities to Children

When your children start to earn their allowances or commissions, it's time for you to teach them how to become financially responsible.

1. Be a good model to your children: allow your kids involve in your financial transactions. Let them take part in observing you dealing with your budget, how you create and balance your budget, how you pay the utility bills. Keep your kids close when you pay for things in the supermarket or the grocery stores so they could see the process and get familiar with your payment procedures.

2. Change your mind about making purchase decisions: occasionally, allow your kid have a chance to see you change the decision about a buy and explain to them how much money affect our purchasing decisions. Teach them on how to return an item and encourage them to ask you questions about how you use money in life.

3. Guide your children on how to create a budget and protect their assets: teach the kid how to build a budget base on how much they spend and how much they save/ make each month. Plus, educate them on how to keep their properties safe and how to protect information relating to such assets.

4. Guide your kid on how to set a financial goal: when your child gets a little old, help them set a financial goal base on allowance or commission you give them daily/ weekly/ monthly. Teach them how to balance their budget, deduct spending, avoid purchasing unnecessary items, stay focused on the financial goal and achieve the goal in anyhow.

5. Enroll your kid in an educational organization with the help of finance experts. This is a great way help your children become smarter and achievable with their financial goals.

6. Recommend your kid some useful websites on financial literacy for children. This great source of information will help the child enhance the knowledge about money and finance in general.

7. Guide your children on how to set up limits on their spending: explain to them the consequences they may suffer from if they spend over the limit.

8. Teach your child that they should only buy necessary things: make this matter clear by explaining to them that they do not always buy things when shopping, they can just go for window shopping at times.

9. Teach your kid that before they decide to buy an item or a service, they should do research on google to see who is selling the product or service. Guide them to consider whether or not they are socially responsible for the products they sell. Is there any reliable source of news talking about the company or their products?

10. Be open with your kid about your family's current financial situation: Talk to them about what things your family spent on, show your child the family's bills and guide the child how to read the billing statements, then show them the process of paying bills. You can also discuss the family budget with your child when you are trying to teach them how to cut down on unnecessary expenses. For example, turn off the water faucet before they leave the bathroom, turn off lights before they leave home, etc.

11. Guiding your kid on how credit card works and teaching them lessons on how to use credit card responsibly

Teaching Children How To Save Money at A Young Age

Knowledge about saving money cannot be learned in a short span of time; it is a gradual and continuous learning process at the early age.

As parents, we can explain to our children how to save money by inventing a fun piggy bank and name it as "the money-saving a pig." Doing so help remind your child that there's more than one thing they are going to do with their money. The piggy bank is going to sit on your child's bedside table and every time money comes into their life, it's going to ask your child silently *"what do you want to do with that money?" "do you want to save some?"* Don't worry about your child understanding the choice, especially when they are still young. Saving is a concept that may be years away, but here's the real trick. It will teach your child that instead of spending, they should save that money to use when necessary.

Educating your children how to save money at an early age will help them build characters and lay the foundation of being financially responsible ability when they become adults. The sooner they begin to save, the bigger budget they will have to use and invest afterward.

Modeling

As parents, we should model what we teach children about spending habits more often by allowing them to observe what we are doing to master these healthy spending habits, and then, of course, they will be likely to imitate our behaviors. For example, shopping with your kid, visit more than one store, compare the prices and quality of the same items in different stores. Then teach them how to bargain and don't pay full price for anything. Guide them how to ask if you are offered a shopper's card or a discount card if you shop at that store usually, etc. This way will help your kid practice and develop their healthy spending habits. They will become more proactive; planning always thinks ahead before spending money on something so that they would avoid the impulse buying. They know how to look for the best prices and deals so they would partly save their money. They will also have a chance of practice tracking their spending and creating budgets much earlier than their peers.

Introducing kids different types of money like notes, coins, checks, etc. to provide them a visualization of a general picture of the money world. Plus, you can also play simple games about the concept of change to help the kid have basic interactions with money since they are at early ages. Before playing this game, make sure your child has been equipped with a basic counting knowledge already. You can play this game by firstly pretending that you are a customer, and your child is a shop owner. You buy an item at a particular price; then you make payment by giving him/her a note with a value bigger than the original price, you ask him/her give you change. For example, you buy an Apple-with the price of 6 dollars, and you give him/her 10 dollars. Ask them how much you get back as a change? That will be a $4 change, right? Then you switch the role of participant, you are a shop owner and your kid will be a customer, then keep practicing the lesson of change until you see your child master this skill.

You can also practice role-playing games with your child by using fake money. Pretending that you are at a shopping mall, at a restaurant or the grocery, then begin to teach your child about using the money to buy items. Pretending that you are the shop owner and your child is a customer. After playing the role of the proprietor, you switch the position of the client, and your kid will become the shop owner. Keep practicing shopping with your child until they have basic knowledge of selling and buying items. You can make the game more exciting and fun by equipping you child with a fun costume of the shop owner, such as an apron, fun shoes, etc.

Invite your children to participate in family shopping activity. Ask the child to help parents look in the refrigerator and kitchen cabinets to figure out what the family needs to buy for the following week. Together with your child go to the supermarket or the grocery store, ask them to compare the price and pick which one is the best bargain. You can also give them an amount of money and ask them to come up with a list of shopping items. While shopping, hand the kid a calculator to let them know how close the budget is and ask them if you can add more items to the shopping cart.

Together with your child set up a plan for a family vacation, let them figure out the estimated expenses for that vacation including the plane tickets, hotel, rental car/ taxi, food, etc.

Through these activities, your child will have a chance to learn a lot from their mistakes. The earlier they make mistakes, the sooner they could experience the consequences or discomfort of making poor spending decisions. We can also use their money mistakes as teaching moments so they would be wiser in purchasing something they want next time. With your guidance, I believe that your kid will become more mature and smarter in using their money.

Teach Kids How to Spend Money Wisely and Consciously

What are main factors influences to children's spending habits?

It cannot be denied that children's spending habits are mostly influenced by fashion trends, the advertising of media, peer pressure or spiritual beliefs through what they observe and practice daily. As a parent, we should equip our kids with essential knowledge, help them understand and be smart about what they are going to spend money on, guide them how to make right choices and decisions when they're buying items.

Be aware that a kid might experience from the peer pressure when half of their classmates possess the latest gadgets or fashion trends. Most of the peers wear the same name-brand clothing, athletic shoes, watches, etc. It's, therefore, highly likely to place your kid in a position of being a social outcast. As parents, you must know how to teach your child how to become a conscious consumer by providing them with knowledge, information, critical skills so that they would become smarter with their budget. You can instill to your child to think and ask fundamental questions before buying items such as *"Do I need it?" "Is it worth the money?" "Is this a long-term or short-term purchase?"*

With that being said, parents must explain to their children about the difference of needs from wants.

1. NEED: a need is something kids must have to survive and grow.

The categories of needs include food, drinks, basic clothing, utilities, and items that improve the child's intelligence, and skills. Also, help them with schoolwork like a calculator, flash cards or books, or a type of musical instrument like a piano, guitar, organ, flute, drum or art supplies, cookware, etc.

2. **WANT:** a want is something kids would like to have, but it's not a big deal if they don't get it. All other items that fall out of the categories of *needs* are considered *wants*.

Together with your kid do the practical exercise of distinguishing between the needs and the wants. Use a white board or take a blank sheet of paper and label two columns: one column for needs and one column for wants. Call out different items in the houses and ask the kid write down all which ones belong to the category of NEEDS, which ones belong to the category of WANTS.

Set Goals

In life, doing anything without a goal or understanding why you're doing this is quite annoying. And if it is boring, you're not going to stick with it. It's crucial that your child sticks with the choice that they make, so keep it fascinating. Help your child set a goal with the decision they have done.

Teach your children on how to set their money goal by using three categories: SAVING, SPENDING, and GIVING. You can use 3 fun piggy banks or 3 mason jars and draw pictures or label on them so your kid could differentiate the money they put into each different category. You can guide them to find a bigger piggy bank or larger jar for the saving, a smaller piggy bank or jar for spending, and a normal one for giving.

1. **SAVING:** guide your kid how to write a financial goal about how much they would like to save in the next one, two, three weeks and display it on the kid's bedroom wall, the desk or somewhere else in the house where the child can see it regularly. For example, I will save $20 by June 30th, $30 by July 7th, etc.
2. **SPENDING:** guide your kid to make a list of things for shopping at school, and you must be strict with them about foods for breakfast, lunch, drinks, study tools, etc. Doing so will help them always consider carefully before buying items.
3. **GIVING:** encourage your kid to give an amount of their saving money on charity in school, church or local orphanage. Teach them that giving should come from the heart, not from being forced to do.

Once your kid accomplishes these 3 above categories, be sure to celebrate them with a small cake, or dinner prepared with their favorite food

When your child grows up to an appropriate age, encourage them to get a part-time job after school-time to earn extra money instead of getting an allowance from parents. This way will not only teach them about to make, manage their money but also manage their time.

Allow them to open a saving account so they would have another place to keep the money for a long term. Let them know the benefits of opening a bank account and how much interest they will accumulate with that amount of money.

Help Your Kid Obtain a Bank Credit Card

You should spend time shopping around and look for the best credit card offering for your child. Try to look for a credit card with the lower interest rate, the better. This is imperative because the interest rate will partly affect the "price" of the money your kids might borrow in future. Therefore, it would be great if you get a credit card with the lowest interest rate.

You may consider co-signing for your kid's credit card. This might give your child a proper consideration when using a credit card for shopping. Of course, as a person who co-sign for the credit card, you will be responsible if your kid doesn't pay a sum of money that is due every month. This way will help you have a chance to know if your child is good at or careful with using a credit card or not, then you can come up with a method to adjust them. Once your child obtains a credit card, you must teach them how to use it effectively since they are a new credit card user. This will help the child avoid using the card wrongly or spending a lot on unnecessary things.

Teaching Children about the Pros and Cons of a Credit Card Usage

Pros

- A credit card will help people be able to buy things or services in an emergency when their cash is not enough on hand or not available.

- With a credit card, people don't have to carry cash, but they are still able to purchase things. Credit cards help them reduce the possibility of losing money or being stolen.

- Some companies will only accept payment via credit card as a way of making a transaction.

Cons

- Apart from they have to pay the amount of money for their bill each month, they also have to pay interest on the balance

- People may spend more money buying things with a credit card than in cash

Explaining the Danger of Credit Card Usage to Children

Credit card organizations tend to target their marketing to teens for their business since they know that many teens are yet equipped knowledge about credit card debt. Statistics show that teenagers often buy things that they do not need. Children are tempted to buy new goods through social media advertising, commercials, TV, especially peer pressure that are equipped things in latest fashion by their parents. As parents, therefore, you must teach your children about this issue or they will be facing financial troubles afterward.

Teach your children on how to do research for information about the national debt average, interest rates. Show them the figures of how much credit card companies earn each year. Tell them sad stories of thousands, even millions of people who are losing their hard-earned pennies to these credit card companies. This is quite unfair, right? The sooner you teach them, the wiser they become about their choices.

Guiding Children on How Credit Card Works and How to Use It Responsibly

We should give our children a brief overview to explain how credit cards work. Teach them that when they use a credit card, it means they're borrowing money from the bank, and will create debt. They will also have to repay it without negotiation. Let them know that when they refund the money to the bank/ credit card company, they always have to pay back more than the amount they were given, because they have to pay an additional amount of interest. The interest will be high or low depending on the terms of the credit card company where the card was released. Teach the kid the responsibility of using their credit card. They must be disciplined with themselves; they must always consider before they buy any items. If possible, parents may practice using credit cards for shopping activities with kids for several times, and then let them do it alone later.

Teaching Children about the Difference between Good Debt and Bad Debt

GOOD DEBT is an amount of money that people borrow to buy an asset as an investing activity like a real estate loan, a business opening loan which will increase the value of assets and allow people to earn more money than they would if they do not have a good debt.

BAD DEBT is an amount of money that people borrow to buy an asset that will lose the value right after it is purchased, like a car loan, a computer loan, or using credit to buy clothes, mobile phones, home utilities, etc.

Credit Card Management: Wise Minimization of Debts

Raise your child awareness of the marketing temptation through online ads, commercials. Doing so will help your children avoid purchasing things they don't need. Encourage them to partake in activities that contribute to raising our kid's consciousness and limit their influence to marketing tactics. Teach your children never use a credit card to buy basic needs like clothing, food, drinks. This is an indication showing that they are using money unwisely.

As parents, you can also warn your children that they never use a credit card to buy things they really can't afford. Tell your kid that if they want to have it, they must work for it by doing chores to get commissions or get a part-time job to earn extra money, then buy it later when they save enough money.

Teach your kid that they should limit the number of credit cards, the more credit cards they possess, the more they can be charged. Encourage them to cut down on the number of credit cards to avoid facing with unexpected debts

Teaching Children How To Check Financial Accounts

Checking financial accounts (bank statements, proof of billings, and the like) are complicated to some adults, more so, to the youth. That is why it is important to teach children how to check financial accounts at a young and reasonable age.

Having said that, start a conversation with your child about the financial issues when they become mature, guide them on how to check accounts properly. This way will help them develop their ability and skills in managing their money and their healthy spending habits as well.

Explain to the kid that the bank or credit card companies will keep their money safe, let them know that they shouldn't carry a lot of cash along with them any time they go shopping. It's perilous, and it may be lost or stolen easily. Encourage them to use a credit card to make a purchase instead of cash.

Financial Knowledge and Safety Measures

Equip your children with valuable knowledge of using credit cards or debit cards safely. Giving them some useful advice so they could prevent themselves from evil or illegal activities that may take place when they're using credit cards at the ATM. Warn them never show anyone their credit card's PIN to anyone, even that is their close friends. Tell them never use an ATM until they find out no one is around. Tell them never stand outside an ATM or in public places and count their cash. It's perilous. Instead, recommend them going to a security area and then count it.

Teaching Children about Taxes

Teaching your children about taxes is also an important concept when they learn about money and finance. Let them know that government and public services need large amounts of money to develop a community; they need people to share burden or contribution for needs of society like education facilities (schools, educational institutions), medical facilities (hospitals, clinics, etc.), traffic facilities (roads, streets, bridges). Therefore, it requires contributions from citizens, and that contribution is called "tax payment." Introduce kids the names, definitions, and functions of different types of taxes including Medicare taxes, sales tax, property tax, inheritance tax, capital gains tax, social security tax, and income tax).

Introducing the Significance of Stocks to Kids at an Early Age

You can buy a stock for your children at the company that they're in. For example, if your kids are playing video games Electronic Arts, then you purchase a stock of Electronic Arts, or if your child likes eating at McDonald's, then you buy a McDonald's stock for them. Or maybe, there are some cool shoes she wears like Nike; then you buy Nike. Perhaps, they're into Disney, then you going purchase a stock of Disney. All in all, it should be something that the kids are excited about.

CONCLUSION

When children learn things, we send them to school, but the things are imperative like their teachers almost never teach money. There's no curriculum to teach them about how to handle their money. Therefore, the task of education the kids about the concept and value of money lie within you as the parent. You are teaching them about money terms and earning, saving, giving and spending habits from the first moment they can see and hear you. Note that they will model you for everything, so make sure you are illustrating the best education about money habits so they would adapt effectively. The best idea is to start teaching money when they are still young. Children also learn from practice. Take time to teach them through exciting games or successful stories of billionaires. Doing so will instill effective money management and develop their entrepreneurial mindset. You need to teach them how to save their money, how to spend their money and how to give with their money as well. These skills will provide them with a variety of opportunity to make their financial status and life more successful in future.

Thank you again for downloading this book on *"Smart Kids Smart Money: The Ultimate Parent's Guide To Teaching Kids About Earning, Saving, Giving, Spending And Investing Money Wisely."* and reading all the way to the end. I'm extremely grateful.

If you know of anyone else who may benefit from the informative tips presented in this book, please help me inform them of this book. I would greatly appreciate it.

Finally, if you enjoyed this book and feel that it has added value to your life in any way, please take a couple of minutes to share your thoughts and post a REVIEW on Amazon. Your feedback will help me to continue to write the kind of Kindle books that helps you get results. Furthermore, if you write a simple REVIEW with positive words for this book on Amazon, you can help hundreds or perhaps thousands of other readers who may want to enhance their life have a chance getting what they need. Like you, they worked hard for every penny they spend on books. With the information and recommendation you provide, they would be more likely to take action right away. We really look forward to reading your review.

Thanks again for your support and good luck!

If you enjoy my book, please write a POSITIVE REVIEW on amazon.

-- Lucy Love --

CHECK OUT OTHER BOOKS

Go here to check out other related books that might interest you:

Marriage Heat: 7 Secrets Every Married Couple Should Know On How To Fix Intimacy Problems, Spice Up Marriage & Be Happy Forever

https://www.amazon.com/dp/B01ITSW8YU

Legal Vocabulary In Use: Master 600+ Essential Legal Terms And
Phrases Explained In 10 Minutes A Day

http://www.amazon.com/dp/B01L0FKXPU

English Collocations In Use: Master 500+ Collocations Explained In 10 Minutes A Day

http://www.amazon.com/dp/B01JHUNYZQ

Shortcut To Ielts Writing: The Ultimate Guide To Immediately Increase Your Ielts Writing Scores

http://www.amazon.com/dp/B01JV7EQGG

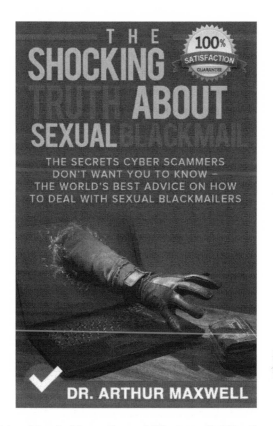

**The Shocking Truth About Sexual Blackmail: The Secrets Cyber
Scammers Don't Want You To Know - The World's Best Advice On
How To Deal With Sexual Blackmailers**

http://www.amazon.com/dp/B01IO1615Y

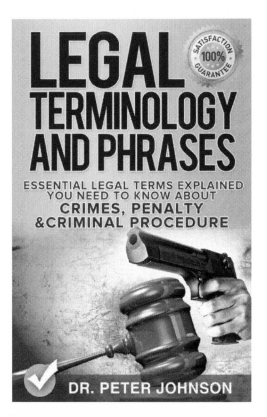

Legal Terminology And Phrases: Essential Legal Terms Explained
You Need To Know About Crimes, Penalty And Criminal Procedure

http://www.amazon.com/dp/B01L5EB54Y

**Legal Terminology And Phrases: Essential Legal Terms Explained
You Need To Know About Civil Law And Civil Procedure**

https://www.amazon.com/dp/B01LDLRU0C

Daughter of Strife: 7 Techniques On How To Win Back Your Stubborn Teenage Daughter

https://www.amazon.com/dp/B01HS5E3V6

Parenting Teens With Love And Logic: A Survival Guide To Overcoming The Barriers Of Adolescence About Dating, Sex And Substance Abuse

https://www.amazon.com/dp/B01JQUTNPM

Productivity Secrets For Students: The Ultimate Guide To Improve Your Mental Concentration, Kill Procrastination, Boost Memory And Maximize Productivity In Study

http://www.amazon.com/dp/B01JS52UT6

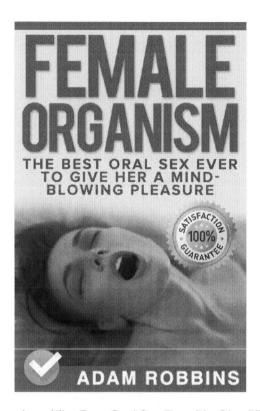

Female Organism: The Best Oral Sex Ever To Give Her A Mind-Blowing Pleasure

https://www.amazon.com/dp/B01KIOVC18